A BOOK OF IRISH INSULTS

For Declan O'Kelly

Mercier Press
PO Box 5 5 French Church Street Cork
16 Hume Street Dublin 2
Trade enquiries to CMD Distribution 55A Spruce Ave
Stillorgan Industrial Park Blackrock County Dublin

First published 1997
© Introduction Sean McMahon 1997. The acknowledgements
page is an extension of this copyright notice

A CIP record for this book is available from the British Library.
ISBN 1 85635 162 9
10 9 8 7 6 5 4 3 2 1

Cover cartoon by Aongus Collins; cover design by Bluett
Typeset by Richard Parfrey
Printed in Ireland by ColourBooks Baldoyle Dublin 13

A BOOK OF IRISH INSULTS

SEAN McMAHON

MERCIER PRESS

ACKNOWLEDGEMENTS

For permission to reprint copyright material, grateful acknowledgement is made to the following:

Tessa Sayle Agency for extracts from *The Hostage* (© Brendan Behan 1958), *Brendan Behan's Island* (© Brendan Behan 1962) and *Borstal Boy* (© Brendan Behan 1958); HarperCollins Publishers for the extract from *The Poor Mouth*, 1973, by Myles na Gopaleen); Maurice Craig for 'Ballad to a Traditional Refrain' (© Maurice Craig); Andre Deutsch Ltd. for the extract from *The Price of My Soul* © 1969 Bernadette Devlin; O'Brien Press for the extract from *As I Was Going Down Sackville Street* by Oliver St John Gogarty; Mercier Press Ltd for the extract from *The Old Munster Circuit* by Maurice Healy, 1939; Robert Harbinson for the extract from *No Surrender* (© Robert Harbinson 1960); Sinclair Howard Jones for 'Hibernia' ; the trustees of the Estate of Patrick Kavanagh, c/o Peter Fallon, Literary Agent, Loughcrew, Oldcastle, County Meath for 'Memory of Brother Michael', extract from *A Soul for Sale*, 1947, and 'The Paddiad or The Devil as a Patron of Irish Letters', 1949; Mercier Press Ltd for the extract from *Sive* © 1959 by John B. Keane; Colbert Kearney on behalf of the estate of Peadar Kearney for 'Whack Fol the Diddle' by Peadar Kearney; the author c/o Rogers, Coleridge & White, 20 Powis Mews, London 11 1JN for the extract from *Poor Lazarus* by Maurice Leitch; David Higham Associates for the extract from *The Poetry of W. B. Yeats*, 1941, and extracts from *Eclogue from Iceland*, 1936 and *Autumn Journal, XVI*, 1938 from the *Collected Poems of Louis MacNeice* edited by E. R. Dobbs and published by Faber & Faber; Gallery Press for the extract from *A Crucial Week in the Life of a Grocer's Assistant*, 1969, by Tom Murphy; Brandon Book Publishers Ltd. for the extract from *Father Ralph*, © 1913, by Gerald O'Donovan; The National Theatre Society Ltd. for the extract from *A Young Man from the South*, © 1917, by Lennox Robinson; The Society of Authors on behalf of the Bernard Shaw Estate for extracts from *Immaturity*, 1879, *The Man of Destiny*, 1897, *O'Flaherty VC*, 1915, *Table Talk of GBS*, *John Bull's Other Island*, 1906 by Bernard Shaw; extracts from 'The Martins of Ross', *Irish Yesterdays*, 1917, 'Philippa's Fox-Hunt', *Some Experiences of an Irish RM* (1899), *The Real Charlotte*, 1894, © Somerville and Ross, reproduced by permission of the Curtis Brown Group Ltd, London; an extract from a a letter to Nancy Mitford, 1952, by Evelyn Waugh reprinted by permission of the Peters Fraser & Dunlop Group Ltd; A. P. Watt Ltd for extracts from 'All Things Can Tempt Me' and 'Remorse for Intemperate Speech' both taken from *The Collected Poems of W. B. Yeats*; .

Every attempt has been made to get in touch with copyright holders. The Publishers regret any errors or omissions in this acknowledgements notice and will be happy to rectify them in future editions.

CONTENTS

Introduction

My dictionary defines the noun 'insult' as 'an offensive remark or action; abuse; an affront; injury; damage (*med esp. US)*'. (Dylan Thomas was diagnosed as having died from an 'insult to the brain' in 1952; the American doctors were polite enough not to add 'self-inflicted'.) The dictionary helpfully adds that its root meaning is to 'leap upon'. The insults in this book may be taken as a collection of Irish verbal 'leps-upon', both actively (as when living up to the foreign insult that we are a belligerent race) and passively (as when these leps are made on us not only by the same insulting foreigners but also with Exocet accuracy by ourselves).

Except for output towards or input from our dear sister Britain, the personalities attacked or attacking are all Irish; and the places, indeed the traits, are all held within latitudes 51.5°–55.5°N and longitudes 5.5°–11°W. Some of the comments may, perhaps, not seem very insulting; in a comparable book published in England the only Irish entry is Lloyd George's description of dealing with de Valera as 'trying to pick up mercury with a fork', which many then and since have taken as an unalloyed compliment. Perhaps for the purpose of this collection of savage wit our definition of 'insult' should be meiotic: remarks and descriptions not intended as complimentary. An element of wit or justifiable rage is essential if insult is not to degenerate into mindless abuse, which is a mark not of grudging respect and worthy enmity but of hatred.

The categories are arbitrary and far from watertight, and entries within have been given in chronological order of perpetrators. Most are factual and in the public domain but some insults from fiction were too sharp to resist. Fiction about Ireland or by Irish authors is surely as Irish as the contents of 'Sayings of the Week' columns in newspapers and periodicals, and it would be an insult to the reader's intelligence to suggest otherwise. The compilation may not include your favourite piece of swinge or, contrariwise, may contain entries which you don't think abusive at all. As ever, the editor is limited in his choice by space, knowledge and idiosyncrasy. In this matter one can only quote a fine wielder of insult, not Irish, to the effect that anthologies (and judgements) are like Pope's watches:

'Tis with our judgements as our watches, none
Go just alike, yet each believes his own.

My thanks are due to Aongus Collins for valuable suggestions.

All versions of Irish or Latin entries are by the compiler, except when otherwise stated.

This Lovely Land

SIR ROBERT CECIL (*c.* 1563–*c.* 1612)
The land of Ire.

Letter to the Lord Admiral, 8 October 1600

WILLIAM SHAKESPEARE (1564–1616)
'Tis like the howling of Irish wolves against the moon.

Rosalind to Orlando in *As You Like It*: V, ii, 104–5, 1599

Of my Nation? What ish my Nation? Ish a villain, and a
bastard, and a knave, and a rascal. What ish my nation? Who
talks of my Nation?

MacMorris in *Henry V*: III, ii, 110–12, 1598

WILLIAM LITHGOW (*fl.* 1614–32)
And this I dare avow, there are more rivers, lakes, brooks,
strands, quagmires, bogs and marshes in this country than
in all Christendom . . . I was never before reducted to such
a floating labyrinth, considering that in five months' space
I quite spoiled six horses, and myself as tired as the worst
of them.

Rare Adventures and Painful Peregrinations

JONATHAN SWIFT (1667–1745)
I reckon no man is thoroughly miserable unless he be
condemn'd to live in Ireland.

Letter to Ambrose Philips, 30 October 1709

Ireland is not Paradise.

Letter to Alexander Pope, 30 August 1716

> He gave the little wealth he had,
> To build a house for fools and mad:
> And showed by one satiric touch,
> No nation wanted it so much.

'Verses on the Death of Dr Swift, DSPD', 1731

GEORGE BERKELEY, DEAN OF DERRY AND BISHOP OF CLOYNE (1685–1754)

Some queries proposed to the consideration of the public:

Whether there be upon earth any Christian or civilised people so beggarly and destitute, as the common Irish?

Whether any countrymen are not readier at finding excuses rather than remedies?

Whether the natural phlegm of this island needs any additional stupifier?

Whether there be not every year more cards circulated at the card tables of Dublin than at all the fairs of Ireland?

The Querist, 1735

REV SYDNEY SMITH (1771–1845)

They do nothing in Ireland as they would elsewhere. When the Dublin mail was stopped and robbed my brother declares that a sweet female voice was heard behind the hedge, exclaiming, 'Shoot the gintlemen then, Patrick dear!'

In Lady Holland, *Memoir of Sydney Smith*, 1855

THOMAS MOORE (1779–1852)
A beautiful country, sir, to live out of!

Attrib.

THOMAS CARLYLE (1795–1881)
Ugly spectacle: sad health: sad humour: a thing unjoyful to look back upon. The whole country figures in my mind like a ragged coat; one huge beggar's gaberdine, not patched, nor patchable any longer.

Journal, 11 November 1849

THOMAS HOOD (1799–1845)
To Scotland Ireland is akin
In drinking like as twin to twin, –
When others' means are all adrift,
A liquor-shop is Pat's last shift,
Till reckoning Erin round from store to store,
There is one whisky shop in four.

'Ode to J. S. Buckingham Esq.', 1835

BENJAMIN DISRAELI (1804–81)
[Ireland] the bane of England and the opprobrium of Europe.

Speech, 9 August 1843

WILLIAM MAKEPEACE THACKERAY (1811–63)
As there is more rain in this country than in any other, and as, therefore, naturally, the inhabitants should be inured to the weather, and made to despise an inconvenience which

11

they cannot avoid, the travelling conveyances are arranged so that you may get as much practice in being wet as possible.

The Irish Sketch Book, 1843

JAMES ANTHONY FROUDE (1818–94)
Order is an exotic in Ireland. It has been imported from England, but it will not grow. It suits neither soil nor climate.

The Two Chiefs of Dunboyne, 1889

WILLIAM ALLINGHAM (1824–89)
History of Ireland – lawlessness and turbulency, robbery and oppression, hatred and revenge, blind selfishness everywhere – no principle, no heroism. What can be done with it?

Diary, 11 November 1866

SOMERVILLE & ROSS
[EDITH OENONE SOMERVILLE (1858–1949)
AND VIOLET MARTIN 1862–1915)]
Christopher, having cut the grocer's cake, and found it was the usual conglomerate of tallow, saw-dust, bad eggs, and gravel, devoted himself to thick bread and butter.

The Real Charlotte, 1894

W[ILLIAM] B[UTLER] YEATS (1865-1939)
   . . . my fool-driven land

'All Things Can Tempt Me', 1910

That is no country for old men.

'Sailing to Byzantium', 1927

Out of Ireland have we come,
Great hatred, little room . . .

'Remorse for Intemperate Speech', 1931

OLIVER ST JOHN GOGARTY (1878–1957)
Nobody can betray Ireland: it does not give him the chance;
it betrays him first.

As I Was Going Down Sackville Street, 1937

MONK GIBBON (1896–1987)
I am from Ireland,
The sad country,
Born, as can be proved,
In her chief city.
I heard much slander
Touching her, from goose
And hissing gander.

'Dispossessed Poet', 1929

LOUIS MACNEICE (1907–63)
I come from an island, Ireland, a nation
Built upon violence and morose vendettas.
My diehard countrymen like drayhorses
Drag their ruin behind them.

Eclogue from Iceland, 1936

Why should I want to go back
To you, Ireland, my Ireland?
The blots on the the page are so black
That they cannot be covered with shamrock.

Autumn Journal, XVI, 1938

STUART HOWARD-JONES (1904–74)

'And now the Irish are ashamed,' Andrew Marvell

MARVELL! I think you'd neither seen nor smelt
In person, the abominable Celt.
No sense of smell he'll find, whoever seeks,
Twixt *Kingstown* and *Magillicuddy's Reeks*,
As CROMWELL knew, who had these *Apemen*
   daily
Clocked smartly on the head with a *Shillelagh*.

Observe the Irishman at night in bed:
His bloodshot eyes are popping from his head,
For there he sees, of blackest Midnight born,
A fearful *Banshee* or *Leprechaun*,
Or other of this pious Country's demons –
The nat'ral fruit of slight *Delirium Tremens*:
And what's this incubus that looms so big
Upon his chest? – Only – Praise God! – the Pig!
Last night he had put down too much *Potheen*
(A vulgar blend of Methyl and Benzene)
That, at some Wake, he might the better keen.

(Keen – meaning 'brisk'? Nay, here the Language
  warps:
'Tis singing bawdy ballads to a Corpse.)
Next day our Irishman goes out of doors
And, pushing through the usual crowd of Whores,
Enters the Church in spirituous Depression
To seek the Priest and make a full Confession:
A useful traffic, for he tells of all
The Tarts he's laid at last night's Funeral,
And thus the Priest can add, perhaps, a name
To his *Compendium* of Easy Game,
While PADRAIC, with his spirit cleansed of sin,
Goes out a better man than he came in.
Then, off to milk his Sow for *Irish Dairies*,
Gets through his penitential Ave Maries
And, with a final gabbled *Decalogue*,
Trips and is swallowed in the treach'rous Bog,
And freed from sin, if not precisely shriven,
Goes up to join the BORGIAS in Heaven,
The while his friends, as if their hearts would
  break,
Lay in the Liquor for another Wake.

Then hear sung, MARVELL, by a wiser Muse,
This land of Popes and Pigs and Bogs and Booze,
For Lycidas (and Milton makes in plain)
Preferred to drown than visit it again.

'Hibernia'

15

Evelyn Waugh (1903–66)

Among the countless blessings I thank God for, my failure
to find a house in Ireland comes first . . . The peasants are
malevolent. All their smiles are false as hell. Their priests
are very suitable for them but not for foreigners. No coal at
all. Awful incompetence everywhere. No native capable of
doing the simplest job . . .

Letter to Nancy Mitford, 1 May 1952

Patrick Kavanagh (1904–67)

Culture is always something that was,
Something pedants can measure,
Skull of bard, thigh of chief,
Depth of dried-up river.
Shall we be thus for ever?
Shall we be thus for ever?

'Memory of Brother Michael', *A Soul for Sale*, 1947

John Broderick (1927–89)

The city dweller who passes through a country town, and
imagines it sleepy and apathetic is very far from the truth:
it is as watchful as the jungle.

The Pilgrimage, 1961

THE MOST DISAGREEABLE
PLACE IN EUROPE

OCTAVIAN DEL PALATIO,
ARCHBISHOP OF ARMAGH (APPOINTED 1480)

> *Civitas Ardmachana,*
> *Civitas vana,*
> *Absque bonis moribus;*
> *Mulieres nudae,*
> *Carnes crudae,*
> *Paupertas in aedibus.*

> [Armagh folk – what a pity!
> Think their wee town's a city
> And with rudeness are patently swellin';
> Their women go bare,
> They eat their meat rare
> And their hovels are not fit to dwell in.]

(As the next entry shows, this view had a lot of currency.)

ANON (SIXTEENTH CENTURY)
An Italian Frier comming of old into Ireland, and seeing at
Armach this their diet and nakednesse of the woman . . . is
said to have cried out,

Civitas Armachana, Civitas vana
Carnes crudae, mulieres nudae

[Vaine Armach City, I did thee pity,
Thy meate rawnes, and womens nakednesse.]

In Fynes Moryson, *An Itinerary*, 1617

ANON (SEVENTEENTH CENTURY)
Jew, Turk or atheist
May enter here
But not a Papist

. . .

Whoever wrote this wrote it well
For the same is writ on the gates of hell.

[Notice alleged to have appeared on one of the gates of Bandon,
County Cork, and the riposte.]

OLIVER CROMWELL (1599–1658)
[Of the Burren, County Clare] There is not wood enough
to hang a man, nor water enough to drown him, nor earth
enough to bury him in.

Attrib. (*c.* 1649–50)

JONATHAN SWIFT (1667–1745)
No men in Dublin go to Taverns who are worth sitting with.

Letter to Charles Ford, 16 August 1725

This town [Dublin] . . . I believe is the most disagreeable
place in Europe, at least to any but those who have been

accustomed to it from their youth, and in such a case I suppose a jail might be tolerable.

Letter to Knightly Chetwode, 23 November 1727

Cork indeed was a place of trade, but for some years past is gone into decay, and the wretched merchants instead of being dealers, are dwindled to pedlars and cheats.

Letter to Lady Brandreth, 30 June 1732

High church, low steeple,
Dirty streets, proud people.

[About Newry, County Down, attrib.]

ANON (EIGHTEENTH CENTURY)

Tá blas gan ceart ag an Muimhneach;
Tá ceart gan blas ag an Ultach;
Níl ceart ná blas ag an Laighneach;
Tá ceart agus blas ag an gConnactach.

[The Munsterman's speech has tune but no rigour;
The Ulsterman is accurate but tuneless;
The Leinsterman's speech has neither one nor the
    other;
The Connachtman has both, without any bother.]
We are the boys that take delight in
Smashing the Limerick lamps when lighting,
Through the streets like sporters fighting
And tearing all before us.

'Garryowen', 1775

JOHN BOYLE
FIFTH EARL OF ORRERY AND CORK (1707–62)
The Scene of Cork is ever the same: dull, insipid, and void of all Amusement.

Letter to Jonathan Swift, 15 March 1737

DR SAMUEL JOHNSON (1709–84)
Dublin though a place much worse than London, is not so bad as Iceland.

Letter to Mrs Christopher Smart, 1791

Boswell: Is the Giant's causeway worth seeing?
Johnson: Worth seeing? yes; but not worth going to see.

Boswell, *Life of Johnson*, 12 October 1779

THE CHEVALIER DE LATOCNAYE
(JOSEPH LOUIS DE BOUGRENET) (1768–?)
I arrived at Cork, the dullest and dirtiest town which can be imagined. The people met with are yawning, and one is stopped every minute by funerals, or hideous troops of beggars, or pigs which run the streets in hundreds, and yet this town is one of the richest and most commercial in Europe.

A Frenchman's Walk through Ireland 1796–1797, 1798

THOMAS MOORE (1779–1852)
[About Kerry] 'All acclivity and declivity, without the intervention of a single horizontal plane; the mountains all rocks, and the men all savages.'

Quoted in *Journal*, 6 August 1823

SIR CHARLES JAMES NAPIER (1782–1853)
[About Limerick in 1827] I remember nothing good but the pigs and gloves; and nothing pleasant but the women, who were quite delightful, and as wicked as they were pretty: or as women could wish to be.

In Sir William Napier,

Life and Opinions of General Charles James Napier, 1857

THOMAS CARLYLE (1795–1881)
Kildare, as I entered it, looked worse and worse: one of the wretchedest wild villages I ever saw.

Reminiscences of My Journey in Ireland in 1849, 1889

ANON (EARLY-NINETEENTH CENTURY)
    I gazed on the fair one – one eye was a swivel;
        Her nose it was smutty, her hands not too
           clean;
    She told me then that she was broiling a divel
        For which they are famous in Fishamble Lane.
                        [Cork]

CHARLES LEVER (1806–72)

Och, Dublin City, there is no doubtin'
Bates every city upon the say;
'Tis there you'll see O'Connell spoutin'
An' Lady Morgan making tay;
For 'tis the capital of the finest nation,
Wid charmin' pisintry on a fruitful sod,
Fightin' like divils for conciliation,
An' hatin' each other for the love of God.

'Dublin City' (*c.* 1826, attrib.)

ANON (NINETEENTH CENTURY)

There was an elopement down in Mullingar,
But sad to relate the pair didn't get far;
'Oh fly,' said he, 'darling, and see how it feels.'
But the Mullingar heifer was beef to the heels.

'The Mullingar Heifer'

Beauing, belle-ing, dancing, drinking,
Breaking windows, damning,
Ever raking, never thinking
Live the rakes of Mallow.

'The Rakes of Mallow'

PATRICK O'KELLY (1754–?)

Alas! how dismal is my tale!
I lost my watch in Doneraile,
My Dublin watch, my chain and seal,
Pilfered at once in Doneraile.

. . .

May fire and brimstone never fail
    To fall in showers on Doneraile;
May all the leading fiends assail
    The thieving town of Doneraile.

. . .

May beef or mutton, lamb or veal
    Be never found in Doneraile;
But garlic soup and savoury kaile
    Be still the food for Doneraile!

'The Curse of Doneraile', 1808

DR JOHN BRENAN (*fl.* 1812–25)

A Connaught man
Gets all he can;
His impudence never has mist-all.
He'll seldom flatter
But bully and batter
And his talks of his kin and his pistol.

A Munster man
Is civil by plan;
Again and again he'll entreat you;
Though you ten times refuse
He his object pursues
Which nine out of ten times is to cheat you.

An Ulster man
Ever means to trepan;
He watches your eye and opinion;
He'll ne'er disagree
Till his interest it be
And insolence marks his dominion.

A Leinster man
Is all cup and can;
He calls t'other provinces names.
Yet each of them see
When he starts with the three
That his distance he frequently saves.

'Provincial Characteristics', *The Milesian Magazine* 1820

FRANCIS SYLVESTER MAHONY
('FATHER PROUT') (1804–66)

> Mud cabins swarm in this place so charming,
> With sailor garments hung out to dry;
> And each abode is snug and commodious
> With pigs melodious in their straw-built sty.

'The Attractions of a Fashionable Irish Watering Place'
[Passage West, County Cork], 1830

J[AMES] B[ROWN] ARMOUR
('ARMOUR OF BALLYMONEY') (1841–1928)

[Belfast] ... a New Jerusalem created largely by jerry-builders.

Attrib.

HENRY JAMES (1843–1916)

I was deeply moved by the tragic shabbiness of this sinister country.

On visiting Dublin, March 1895

BERNARD SHAW (1856–1950)

... my sentimental regard for Ireland does not include the capital.

Preface to *Immaturity* (1879)

... Dublin, that city of tedious and silly derision ...

Interview in the *Evening Sun*, New York, 9 December 1911

25

SOMERVILLE & ROSS
[EDITH OENONE SOMERVILLE (1858–1949)
AND VIOLET MARTIN (1862–1915)]
An August Sunday in the north side of Dublin. Epitome of
all that is hot, arid, and empty.

The Real Charlotte, 1894

W[ILLIAM] B[UTLER] YEATS (1865–1939)
    You gave, but will not give again
    Until enough of Paudeen's pence
    By Biddy's halfpennies have lain
    To be 'some sort of evidence',
    Before you'll put your guineas down,
    That things it were a pride to give
    Are what the blind and ignorant town
    Imagines best to make it thrive.

'To a Wealthy Man who promised a Second Subscription to the Dublin
   Municipal Gallery if it were proved the People wanted Pictures' (1913)

RICHARD ADAMS (*fl.* 1880–90)
You have now been acquitted by a Limerick jury, and you
may now leave the dock without any further stain on your
character.

In Maurice Healy, *The Old Munster Circuit*, 1939

LENNOX ROBINSON (1886–1958)
Over the flat country north of Maryboro' the watery sunshine
was slanting in narrow yellow streaks. The country there,
hardly desolate enough to be picturesque, has an air of

exhaustion about it which makes it particularly disagreeable
to me.

A Young Man from the South, 1917

PATRICK MACGILL (1890–1963)
God's choice about the company He keeps and never comes
near Derry.

The Rat Pit, 1915

ANON (TWENTIETH CENTURY)
    The bells of Shandon
    Sound so grand on
    The lovely waters of the Lee
    But the bells of St Nicholas
    Sound so ridiculous
    On the dirty waters
    Of Sullivan's Quay.

Rhyme chanted by visiting actors to Cork

ANON (TWENTIETH CENTURY)
The first prize was a week's holiday in Belfast; the second
was a fortnight's holiday.

Popular gibe

DONAGH MACDONAGH (1912–68)
    Bawneen and currach have no allegiance of mine,
    Nor the cute self-deceiving talkers of the South . . .

'Dublin Made Me', *The Hungry Grass*, 1947

The soft and dreary midlands with their tame
   canals
Wallow between sea and sea, remote from
   adventure,
And Northward a far and fortified province
Crouches under the lash of arid censure.

Ibid.

MAURICE JAMES CRAIG *(b.* 1919)
   O the bricks they will bleed and the rain it will
      weep,
   And the damp Lagan fog lull the city to sleep
   It's to hell with the future and live on the past:
   May the Lord in His mercy be kind to Belfast

'Ballad to a Traditional Refrain'

A Fair People

WILLIAM SHAKESPEARE (1564–1616)

Now for our Irish wars.
We must supplant those rough rug-headed kerns
Who live like venom where no venom else
But only they have privilege to live.

Richard II: II, i, 155–8, 1595

FYNES MORYSON (1566–1630)

The wild and (as I may say) meere Irish, inhabiting many
and large Provinces, are barbarous and most filthy in their
diet. They skum the seething pot with a handfull of straw,
and straine their milke taken from the Cow through a
handfull of straw, none of the cleanest, and so clense, or
rather more defile the pot and milke. They devour great
morsels of beefe unsalted, and they eat commonly Swines
flesh, seldom mutton, and all these pieces of flesh, as also
the intralles of beasts unwashed, they seeth in a hollow tree,
lapped in a Cowes hide, and so set over the fier, and thereby
swallow whole lumps of filthy butter.

An Itinerary, 1617

JOHN DERRICKE (*fl.* 1578–1600)

My soul doth detest their wild shamrock manners.

The Image of Irelande, 1581

ANON (SEVENTEENTH CENTURY)

Síoda, ór agus airgead,
Ceol is Laidean na tíre,
do thabhairt do choileán den cuaine;
ní dhéanfaidh sé uasal choiche é.

[Silken clothes, silver and gold,
Music and classical lore
May be lavished upon a young puppy
But he'll still be as crass as before.]

ANDREW MARVELL (1621–78)

And now the Irish are ashamed
To see themselves in one year tamed.

'An Horatian Ode upon Cromwell's Return from Ireland', 1650

DÁIBHÍ Ó BRUADAIR (*c.* 1625–98)

Mairg nach fuil 'na thrudaire
eadraibhse, a daoine maithe,
ós iad is fearr chugaibhse,
a dream gan iúl gan aithne.

[Why shouldn't I be a tongue-tied clod
When I meet you, neighbours?
It's what you're happiest with, by God,
Yahoos, not worth my labours.]

Seirbhíseach seirgthe íogair sronach seasc
d'eitigh sinn is eibear íota in scornain feacht,
beireadh síobhra d'eitill í gan lón tar lear,
an deilbhín gan deirglí nár fhóir mo thart.

[A skivvy who's nasty and nosey and barren
Refused me drink and me with my tongue hanging
    out.
May some bogeyman whisk her lunchless over the
    sea,
That thin-blooded runt who wouldn't succour my
drought.
. . .

Meirgíneach bheirbhthe í gan cheol 'na cab
do theilg sinn le greidimín sa bpóirse amach;
cé cheilim ríomh a peidigraoi mar fhógras reacht,
ba bheag an díth dá mbeireadh sí do ghosta cat.

[A cantankerous slavey with never a tune in her
    gob
That turfed me with kicks o'er the haughty lip of
her porch –
(The law prevents my giving her seed and her
    breed.)
May she bear a cat to a spook and be left in the
    lurch.]

'Seirbhíseach Seirgthe Íogair Srónach Seasc'
'Mairg Nach Bhfuil 'na Dhubhthuatha' ['A Pity Not to Be an Utter Boor']

31

JONATHAN SWIFT (1667–1745)

Whereas the bearer served under me the space of one year, during which time he was an idler and a drunkard, I then discharged him as such; but how his having been five years at sea may have mended his manners, I leave to the penetration of those who may after employ him.

Deanery House, January 9th, 1739

Testimonial supplied to a servant

GEORGE FARQUHAR (1677–1707)

SUBTLEMAN: And how do you intend to live?

TEAGUE: By eating, dear joy, fen I can get it; and by sleeping when I can get none: 'tish the fashion of Ireland.

The Twin Rivals, 1702

ANON (EIGHTEENTH CENTURY)

You haven't an arm and you haven't a leg
You're an eyeless, noseless, chickenless egg;
You'll have to be put with a bowl to beg.

'Johnny, I Hardly Knew Ye'

Aodh Buí Mac Cruitín (*c.* 1680–1775)

An tan téid sin le chéile i scuaine ag ól
ní féidir a n-éisteacht le fuaim a ngeoin'
tan théifid a mbéalaibh i gcuachaibh teo
béidh a ngaol le gach éinne den uaisle is mó.

[When they go out in a mob for a bevy
You're deafened with brattle like bagpipers' skirls
And when they're all legless with jars hot and heavy
They think their relations are barons and earls.

'Do Chlann Tomáis' ['For Clann Thomas' (those Irish who aped

English ways)]

John Winstanley (1678–1750)

When Fatty walks the street the paviors cry,
'God bless you, sir!' and lay their hammers by.

'On a Fat Man', *Poems*, 1742

Dr Samuel Johnson (1709–84)

The Irish are not in a conspiracy to cheat the world by false
representations of the merits of their countrymen. No sir, the
Irish are a fair people; – they never speak well of one another.

Boswell, *Life of Johnson*, 18 February 1775

Richard Twiss (eighteenth century)

As to the natural history of the Irish species, they are only
remarkable for the thickness of their legs, especially those
of plebian females.

Tour in Ireland (1776)

AODH MAC GABHRÁIN (*fl.* 1715)

A ghearráin ler chailleas mo shearc,
gabh an diabhal, is fag m'amharc;
    go mba measa bhias tú bliain ó inniu,
    is dar anam m'athara ní súgra.

[Useless nag, you have cost me the love of my life.
Go to hell, you hack without merit.
    I hope you will sicken and dwindle away.
    By the soul of my father I swear it!]

An bhfuil naíre ort, a ghearráin gan chéill,
a stráidh dhiabhlaí an aiméis,
    m'fhágáil ar mo tharr san gcac,
    is ábhar mo mhná ar m'amharc.

You should surely, fool jade, be deeply ashamed,
You cretin of origin seamy!
    To deliver me prone on a mountain of shit
    In the place where my woman could see me.]

        'Achasán an Mharcaigh' ['The Horseman's Denunciation']

JOHANN WOLFGANG VON GOETHE (1749–1832)

The Irish seem to me like a pack of hounds, always dragging
down some noble stag.

In Johann Peter Eckermann, *Conversations with Goethe,* 1837 [in praise
        of Wellington's stand against Catholic Emancipation]

DUKE OF WELLINGTON (1769–1852)

The Irish militia are useless in times of war and dangerous in times of peace.

Attrib.

SIR WALTER SCOTT (1771-1832)

Their natural disposition is turned to gaiety and happiness: while a Scotchman is thinking about the term-day, or if easy upon that subject, about hell in the next world – while an Englishman is making a little hell in the present, because his muffin is not well roasted – Pat's mind is always turned to fun and ridicule. They are terribly excitable, to be sure, and will murder you on slight suspicion, and find out next day that it was all a mistake, and that it was not yourself they meant to kill at all at all.

Diary, 21 November 1825

ANON (NINETEENTH CENTURY)

When I went to bed at night upon it I would roll,
The fleas they made a strong attack my kidneys
    for to hole,
I shouted holy murder as my skin they tried to tan,
And I'd pray, 'What made me hire with this man
    called Tom McCann?'

'The Hiring-Fair at Hamilton's Bawn'

BENJAMIN DISRAELI (1804–81)

The Irish hate our free and fertile isle. They hate our order, our civilisation, our enterprising industry, our sustained courage, our decorous liberty, our pure religion. This wild, reckless, indolent, uncertain, and superstitious race, have no sympathy with the English character. Their fair ideal of human felicity is an alternation of clannish broils and coarse idolatry. Their history describes an unbroken cycle of bigotry and blood.

Letter to The Times, 1836

THOMAS BABINGTON, LORD MACAULAY (1800–59)

The aboriginal peasantry [of late seventeenth-century Ireland] were in an almost savage state. They never worked till they felt the sting of hunger. They were content with accommodation inferior to that which, in happier countries, was provided for domestic cattle. Already the potato, a root which can be cultivated with scarcely any art, industry, or capital, and which cannot be long stored, had become the food of the common people. For a people so fed diligence and forethought were not to be expected.

History of England, 1849–61

ANTHONY TROLLOPE (1815–82)

We hear much of their spendthrift nature; but extravagance is not the nature of the Irishman. He will count the shillings in a pound much more accurately than an Englishman and will with much more certainty get twelve pennyworth from each. But they are perverse, irrational, and but little bound by the love of truth.

Autobiography, 1880

EDWARD VAUGHAN KENEALY (1819–80)

What is an Irishman but a mere machine for converting potatoes into human nature?

Table Talk, 1875

DION [LARDNER] BOUCICAULT (1820–90)

The fire and energy that consist of dancing around the stage in an expletive manner, and indulging in ridiculous capers and extravagancies of language and gesture, form the materials of a clowning character, known as the 'stage Irishman', which it has been my vocation to, as an artist and as a dramatist, to abolish.

Letter to a newspaper in Christchurch, New Zealand, 1885

WILLIAM ALLINGHAM (1824–89)

An Antrim Presbyterian, short and spare,
Quick, busy, cool; with lancet or with pill
Acknowledged first with Aesculapian skill.
Catholicism he openly despised,
But ailing Papists cleverly advised . . .
'Ireland forsooth, a nation once again!
If Ireland was a nation, tell me when?
For since the civil modern world began
What's Irish History? Walks the child a man?
Or strays he still perverse and immature,
Weak, slothful, rash, irresolute, unsure;
Right bonds rejecting, hugging rusty chains,
Nor one clear view, nor one bold step attains?
What Ireland might have been, if wisely schooled

37

I know not: far too briefly Cromwell ruled.
We see the melting of a barbarous race
(Sad sight, I grant, sir), from their ancient place
But always, everywhere, it had been so
Red-indians, Bushmen, Irish, – they must go!'

Laurence Bloomfield in Ireland, 1864

GEORGE MOORE (1852–1933)

Democratic principles are unsuited to Ireland . . . The Irish
like priests and believe in the power of priests to forgive
them their sins and to change God into a biscuit. They are
only happy in convents and monasteries. The only reason the
Irish would tolerate home rule would be if they were given
permission to persecute somebody, that is the Roman Catholic
idea of liberty. It always has and always will be.

Letter to Edward Marsh, 3 August 1916

M[ICHAEL] J[OSEPH] MACMANUS (1888–1951)

Firm Cuchullain, Brian Boru,
Silken Thomas and Red Hugh,
Are men of whom fine things are said –
But then they are dead.

So This Is Dublin, 1927

R[OBERT] M[AIRE] SMYLLIE (1894–1954)

Troglyditic myrmidons; moronic clodhoppers; ignorant
bosthoons; poor cawbogues whose only claim to literacy was
their blue pencils.

Description of the staff of the Government censorship office during the Emergency, in Dónal Ó Drisceoil, *Censorship in Ireland during the Second World War*, 1996

SEAN O'FAOLAIN (1900–91)

I have, I confess, grown a little weary of abusing our bourgeois, Little Irelanders, chauvinists, puritans, stuffed-shirts, pietists, Tartuffes, Anglophobes, Celtophiles, et *alii hujus generis*.

'Signing Off', *The Bell*, XII, i, April 1946

In Ireland a policeman's lot is a supremely happy one. God smiles, the priest beams, and the novelist groans.

'The Dilemma of Irish Letters', *The Month*, December 1949

JOHN B[RENDAN] KEANE (*b.* 1928)

May he screech with awful thirst
May his brains and eyeballs burst
That melted *amadán*, that big bostoon
May the fleas consume his bed
And the mange eat up his head,
The blackman from the mountain, Seánín Rua.

Sive: II, ii, 1959

WON'T MOTHER ENGLAND
BE SURPRISED!

CHARLES MACKLIN [MCLOUGHLIN] (1690–1797)

SIR PERTINAX MACSYCOPHANT: ... for I observed, sir, that beauty is, generally, a proud vain saucy, expensive, impertinent sort of a commodity.

EGERTON: Very justly observed.

SIR PERTINAX: And therefore, sir, I left it to prodigals and coxcombs that could afford to pay for it; and in its stead, sir, mark – I looked out for an ancient well-jointured, superannuated dowager; a consumptive, toothless, phthisicky, wealthy widow; or a shriveled cadaverous piece of deformity, in the shape of an izzard [the letter Z] or an appersi-and-or [the ampersand: &]; in short anything that had the siller – the siller, for that, sir, was the north star of my affections.

The Man of the World: I, 1781

THOMAS SHERIDAN (1719–88)

Of all the husbands living an Irishman's the best,
No nation on the globe, like him can stand the
    test,
The English are all drones, as you may plainly see,
But we're all brisk and airy and lively as a bee.

The Brave Irishman or Captain O'Blunder: Sc 7, 1743

EDMUND BURKE (1729–97)

... the age of chivalry is gone. That of the sophisters, economists and calculators has succeeded.

Reflections on the Revolution in France, 1790

REV SYDNEY SMITH (1771–1845)

The moment the very name of Ireland is mentioned, the English seem to bid adieu to common feeling, common prudence and common sense, and to act with the barbarity of tyrants and the fatuity of idiots.

Peter Plymley, *Letters*, no 2, 1807

THOMAS MOORE (1779–1852)

I have found a gift for my Erin,
    A gift that will surely content her; –
Sweet pledge of a love so endearing!
    Five millions of bullets I've sent her.

She'd ask'd me for Freedom and Right
    But ill she her wants understood;
Ball cartridges, morning and night,
    Is a dose that will do her more good.

'A Pastoral Ballad, by John Bull', 1827

[written on hearing that after the defeat of Catholic Emancipation five million rounds of bullets were sent to the army in Ireland.]

MARY O'BRIEN (*fl.* 1783–90)

A face! for so the stories run,
Resembling much on a mid-day sun;
Broad chin, plump cheeks ascending rise,
Sinking the twinkling of two eyes:
Such Jacky Bull, so soft and mellow
He's a mere woolsack of a fellow.
With belly not unlike a butt,
Behold him oft in elbow strut,
Discoursing on Britannia laws,
A counsellor in freedom's cause;
As Bacchus on a barrel rides
So he on liberty bestrides,
Trotting with hobby horse's motion
To mount the cliffs of mother ocean.
Firm as a rock, a Briton born,
A foreign coast he views with scorn . . .

'The Freedom of John Bull', 1790

ANON (NINETEENTH CENTURY)

It seems that praties in their skins
    Are not their only food,
And that they have a house or two
    Which is not built of mud.
In fact, they're not all brutes and fools
    And I suspect that when
They rule themselves they'll be as good,
    Almost, as Englishmen!

'The Native Englishman (By a Converted Saxon)'

Oh, well do I remember the bleak December day
The landlord and the sheriff came to drive us all
    away;
They set my roof on fire with their cursed English
    spleen,
And that's another reason why I left old Skibbereen.

'Old Skibbereen'

JAMES CLARENCE MANGAN (1803–49)

I hate thee Djann Bool,
Worse than Marid or Afrit
Or corpse-eating Ghool;
I hate thee like Sin,
For thy mop-head of hair
The snub nose and bald chin,
And thy turkeycock air . . .

'To the Ingleezee Khafir', 1837

LADY FRANCESCA WILDE (1826–96)

We are wretches, famished, scorned, human tools
    to build your pride,
But God will yet take vengeance for the souls for
    whom Christ died.
Now is your hour of pleasure – bask ye in the
    world's caress;
But our whitening bones against ye will rise as
    witnesses,
From the cabins and the ditches in their charred,
    uncoffined masses,

For the Angel of the Trumpet will know them as
    he passes.
A ghastly spectral army, before great God we'll
    stand,
And arraign ye as our murderers, O spoilers of our
    land!

'The Famine Year', The Nation, 1845

OSCAR WILDE (1854–1900)

The English country gentleman galloping after a fox – the
unspeakable in full pursuit of the uneatable.

A Woman of No Importance: I

BERNARD SHAW (1856–1950)

There is nothing so bad or good that you will not find
Englishmen doing it; but you will never find an Englishman
in the wrong. An Englishman does everything on principle:
he fights you on patriotic principle; he robs you on business
principles; he enslaves you on imperial principles; he bullies
you on manly principles; he supports his king on royal
principles and cuts off his king's head on republican principles.

The Man of Destiny, 1897

The British officer seldom likes Irish soldiers; but he always
tries to have a certain proportion of them in his battalion,
because, partly from a want of common sense which leads
them to value their lives less than Englishmen do (lives are
really less worth living in a poor country) and partly because
even the most cowardly Irishman feels obliged to outdo an

Englishman in bravery if possible, and at least to set a perilous pace for him, Irish soldiers give an impetus to these military operations which require for their spirited execution more devilment than prudence.

Preface, O'Flaherty VC, 1915

JOSEPH CAMPBELL (1897–1944)
    The poet loosed a wingèd song
    Against the hulk of England's wrong.
    Were poisoned words at his command
    'Twould not avail for Ireland.

'The Poet Loosed a Wingèd Song', 1907

OLIVER ST JOHN GOGARTY (1878–1957)
'What shall it profit a man, if he shall gain the whole world and lose his own soul?' That must be why England gained the whole world.

Going Native, 1940

ROBERT [WILSON] LYND (1879–1949)
What I especially like about the English is that having called you a thief and a liar and patted you on the back for being so charming in spite of it, they look honestly depressed if you fail to see that they have been paying you a handsome compliment.

Irish and English, 1908

PATRICK H[ENRY] PEARSE (1879–1916)

A French writer has paid the English a well-deserved compliment. He says they have never committed a useless crime.

'The Murder Machine', 1916

PEADAR KEARNEY (1883–1942)

Oh Irishmen forget the past
And think of the day that is coming fast,
When we shall all be civilised,
Neat and clean and well-advised.
Won't Mother England be surprised!

'Whack Fol the Diddle'

ANON (TWENTIETH CENTURY)

I went to see David, to London to David,
I went to see David and what did he do?
He gave me a Free State, a nice little Free State,
A Free State that's tied up with Red, White and
Blue.

'The Irish Free State'

BRENDAN BEHAN (1923–64)

A shrivelled-up seldom-fed bastard that had stolen money from under his dead mother's body and then put his hand on her and sworn he hadn't.

Borstal Boy, 1958

DISTRESSFUL COUNTRY

GIRALDUS CAMBRENSIS (*c.* 1147–*c.* 1223)
This [the Irish] is a sordid people, steeped in vice. Of all
nations it is the least learned in the facts of the Faith.

Topographica Hibernica, 1188

EDMUND SPENSER (*c.* 1522–99)
[The Irish mantle] . . . a fit house for an outlaw, a meet bed
for rebel, and an apt cloak for a thief.

A View of the Present State of Ireland, 1596

In her [the wandering prostitute's] travels it [the mantle] is
her cloak and safeguard and also a coverlet for her lewd
exercise, and when she has filled her vessel, under it she can
hide both her burden and her shame.

Ibid.

THOMAS, FIRST MARQUIS OF WHARTON
(1648–1715)
There was an old prophecy found in a bog,
    Lilli burlero bullen a la
That our land would be ruled by an ass and a dog:
    Lilli burlero bullen a la
So now dis old prophecy's coming to pass,
    Lilli burlero bullen a la

For Talbot's the dog and Tyrconnel's the ass
    Lilli burlero bullen a la

'Lilli Burlero', 1687

COLONEL WILLIAM BLACKER (1777–1855)

He comes, the open rebel fierce – he comes, the
    Jesuit sly;
But put your trust in God, my boys, and keep your
    powder dry.

'Oliver [Cromwell]'s Advice', 1848

RICHARD LALOR SHEIL (1791–1851)

A body of armed Orangemen fall upon and put to death a
defenceless Catholic; they are put on trial, and when they
raise their eyes and look upon the jury as they are commanded
to do, they see twelve of their brethren in massacre.

Speech at Peneden Heath, Kent, October 1828

ANON (EIGHTEENTH CENTURY)

I met wid Napper Tandy and he took me by the
    hand,
And he said, 'How's poor ould Ireland, and how
    does she stand?'
She's the most distressful country that iver yet was
    seen,
For they're hangin' men and women there for the
    wearin' of the green.

'The Wearin' o' the Green' [Boucicault used a version of this in his
play Arrah na Pogue, 1864]

Anon. (early-nineteenth century)

The glorious, pious and immortal memory of the great and good King William: – not forgetting Oliver Cromwell who assisted in redeeming us from popery, slavery, arbitrary power, and wooden shoes. May we never lack a Williamite to kick the **** of a Jacobite! and a **** for the *Bishop of Cork*! And that he won't drink this whether he be priest, bishop, deacon, bellows-blower, gravedigger, or any other of the fraternity of the *clergy*; may a north wind blow him to the south, and a west wind blow him to the east! May he have a dark night – a lee shore – a rank storm – and a leaky vessel, to carry him over the river Styx! May the dog Cerberus make a meal of his rump, and Pluto a snuff-box of his skull; and the devil jump down his throat with a red-hot harrow, with every pin to tear a gut, and blow him with a *clean* carcass to hell! Amen!

Orange toast quoted in Sir Jonah Barrington, *Personal Sketches*, 1832

Cardinal Paul Cullen (1803–78)

As to what is called Fenianism, you are aware that looking on it as a compound of folly and wickedness wearing a mask of patriotism to make dupes of the unwary, and as the work of a few fanatics and knaves, wicked enough to jeopardise others in order to promote their own sordid views, I have repeatedly raised my voice against it since it first became known at McManus's funeral.

Pastoral letter, 10 October 1865

THOMAS DAVIS (1814–45)

'Did they dare, did they dare, to slay Eoghan
    Ruadh O'Neill?'
'Yes, they slew with poison him they feared to
    meet with steel.'
'May God wither up their hearts! May their blood
    cease to flow!
May they walk in living death, who poisoned
    Eoghan Ruadh!'

                'Lament for the Death of Eoghan Ruadh O'Neill', 1842

                                    [the first poem Davis wrote]

REV WILLIAM ALEXANDER, PRIMATE OF ARMAGH
(1824–1911)

Home Rule morally is a great betrayal;
Logically it is a great fallacy.
Religiously a great sectarianism;
Financially a great swindle
Socially a great break up
And imperially a great breakdown.

'Home Rule in a Nutshell', Unionist broadsheet from sermon, 1893

WILLIAM ALLINGHAM (1824–89)

Not men and women in an Irish street
But Catholics and Protestants you meet.

                                                    Attrib.

'BALLYHOOLEY' [ROBERT MARTIN] (*fl.* 1880s)

What is the reason of our ills?
(A question the Saxon shirks) –
Is it the English Government
Or the Irish Board of Works?

'An Alternative'

LORD RANDOLPH [SPENCER] CHURCHILL
(1849-94)

... foul Ulster tories who have always ruined our party.

16 November 1885, quoted in Robert Kee, *The Green Flag* (1972)

JAMES CONNELL (1852–1929)

Oh, we hate the cruel tiger
And hyena and jackal
But the false and dirty blackleg
Is the vilest beast of all.

Broadsheet, Dublin ITGWU strike, August 1913

JANE BARLOW (1857–1917)

The *United Irishman* is wildly seditious and therefore as
delightful to me as a British disaster.

Letter, December 1900

WILLIAM BULFIN (1862–1910)

The high councils of fanatics and schemers, who direct the
No-Popery campaigns, may be said to be in permanent
session [in Belfast].

Rambles in Erin, 1907

SHAN F[ADH] BULLOCK (1865–1935)

In our Colony the Protestant was top dog always, and both
dogs alike could but snap at the conquering Saxon's feet.

By Thrasna River, 1895

SUSAN L[ANGSTAFF] MITCHELL (1866–1926)

God of the Irish Protestant,

You have grown hideous in our sight;

You're not the kind of god we want.

Rise, Sons of William, rise and smite!

New gods we'll serve, and with them yet

We'll get all there is left to get!

'Ode to the British Empire', *Aids to Immortality of Certain Persons*,

1908

John Redmond spake up boldly

'My members, every day

The people look more coldly

On everything we say.

My gift for making speeches

Is rusting with disuse,

Sinn Feiners with their screeches

Will send us to the deuce.'

Ibid. (1913 edition)

SIR WINSTON {LEONARD SPENCER] CHURCHILL (1874–
1964)

The whole map of Europe has been changed . . . but as the
deluge subsides and the waters fall short, we see the dreary

52

spires of Fermanagh and Tyrone emerging once again. The integrity of their quarrel is one of the few institutions that has been unaltered in the cataclysm which has swept the world.

Speech in the House of Commons, 16 February 1922

JAMES [JIM] LARKIN (1876–1947)

It is a scandalous thing that they should disgrace a broken bottle by using it on an officer of the British Army.

12 August 1907, during dock strike, in John Gray, *City in Revolt*, 1985

OLIVER ST JOHN GOGARTY (1878–1957)

Belfast owes us a mighty grudge for not supporting in Dublin that sink of acidity – Lord Carson. He used the enemies of Ireland as a springboard, and is now safely deposited on the English Woolsack.

Speech in Seanad Éireann, 12 December 1922

SIR BASIL BROOKE,
FIRST VISCOUNT BROOKEBOROUGH (1888–1973)

Many in the audience employ Catholics, but I have not one about the place. Catholics are out to destroy Ulster with all their might and power. They want to nullify the Protestant vote, take all they can out of Ulster and then see it go to hell.

Speech at Mulladuff, Newtownbutler, County Armagh, 12 July 1933

We are carrying on a Protestant Parliament for a Protestant people.

Speech at Stormont, 21 November 1934

M[ICHAEL] J[OSEPH] MACMANUS (1888–1951)
William the Third
Looked slightly absurd
But whisper it low
In Sandy Row.

'So This Is Dublin', 1927

TERENCE, LORD O'NEILL OF THE MAINE
(1914–1990)
The people of Londonderry and the people of Ulster would do very ill to exchange their hope of prosperity for a tattered green banner and a snatch of an old song, carried away by the wind.

Speech in Derry, 14 February 1964

It is frightfully hard to explain to a Protestant that if you give Roman Catholics a good job and a good house, they will live like Protestants, because they will see neighbours with cars and television sets.

They will refuse to have eighteen children, but if the Roman Catholic is jobless and lives in a most ghastly hovel, he will rear eighteen children on national assistance ...

If you treat Roman Catholics with due consideration and kindness they will live like Protestants, in spite of the authoritative nature of their Church.

Radio interview reported in the *Belfast Telegraph*, 5 May 1969

REGINALD MAUDLING (1917–79)

For God's sake bring me a large Scotch. What a bloody awful country.

Reported comment on flight back to London, 1 July 1970

ROBERT HARBINSON (*b.* 1928)

Being children of a staunch Protestant quarter, to go near the Catholic idolaters was more than we dared for fear of having one of our members cut off.

No Surrender, 1960

MAURICE LEITCH (*b.* 1933)

The Protestant ruling majority. An ugly race. In-breeding? No poet will ever sing for them – of them.

Poor Lazarus, 1969

LITERARY MOVEMENTS

ANON (SEVENTEENTH CENTURY)

Deirim dán, ón deirim dán,
an tráth bhíos mo bholg lán;
   an uair mach mbíonn mo bholg lán
   don deamhan dán ná amhrán.

[I write my poems, day and night
When I'm eating well
But when the pains of hunger bite
Then my verse can go to hell.]

DÁIBHÍ Ó BRUADAIR (*c.*1625–98)

Nach ait an nós seo ag mórchuid d'fhearaibh Éireann
d'at go nó le mortas maingléiseach!
   Cé tais a dtreoir ar chódaibh Gall-chléire,
   ní chanaid glór gósta garbh-Bhéarla.

[Is it not odd that most men of this island
Turn daft foppish hauteur into a religion!
Though poor be their grasp of the lore of the nigh
   land
The English they speak – it is babu or pidgin!]

'Nach ait' ['Is it not odd?']

SIR RICHARD STEELE (1672–1729)

We were some little time fixed in our seats, and sat with that dislike which people not too good-natured usually conceive of each other at first sight.

The Spectator, no. 132, 1 August 1711

EDMUND BURKE (1729–97)

Because half a dozen grasshoppers under a fern make the field ring with their important chink, whilst thousands of great cattle, reposed beneath the shadow of the British oak, chew the cud and are silent, pray do not imagine that those who make the noise are the only inhabitants of the field – that, of course, they are many in number – or that, after all, they are other than the little shrivelled, meagre, hopping, though loud and troublesome insects of the hour.

Reflections on the Revolution in France, 1790

RICHARD BRINSLEY SHERIDAN (1751–1826)

A circulating library in a town is an ever-green tree of diabolical knowledge! It blossoms through the year.

The Rivals: I, ii, 1775

JOHN O'LEARY (1830–1907)

It is one among the many misfortunes of Ireland that she has never yet produced a great poet.

Lecture in Cork, February 1886

T[HOMAS] P[OWER] O'CONNOR (1848–1929)

Our old acquaintance enables me to say that all your suggestions [for articles for *T. P.'s Weekly*] turn my stomach. They reek of Fleet Street.

Letter to Augustine Birrell (1850–1933),
Chief Secretary for Ireland (1907–16), *c.* 1902

SARAH PURSER (1848–1943)

Gentlemen kiss and never tell. Cads kiss and tell. George [Moore] doesn't kiss but he tells.

Attrib.

GEORGE [AUGUSTUS] MOORE (1852–1933)

His [Douglas Hyde's] volubility was as extreme as a peasant's come to ask for a reduction of rent. It was interrupted by Edward [Martyn] calling on him to speak in Irish, and then a torrent of dark stuff flowed from him, much like the porter which used to be brought up from Carnacun to be drunk by the peasants on Midsummer nights when a bonfire was lighted.

Hail and Farewell: Ave, 1911

BERNARD SHAW (1856–1950)

I could not write the words Mr Joyce uses: my prudish hands would refuse to form the letters.

Table Talk of GBS, 1906

JANE BARLOW (1857–1917)

That old yahoo George Moore . . . His stories impressed me
as being on the whole like gruel spooned up off a dirty floor.

Letter, November 1914

AMANDA MCKITTRICK ROS (1860–1939)

Here lies a blooming rascal
Once known as Jamie Jarr;
A lawyer of the lowest type,
Who loved your name to char.
Of clownish ways and manners,
He aped at speaking fine,
Which proved as awkward to him
As a drawing-room to swine.

'Jamie Jarr', Poems of Puncture, 1912

His snout is long with a flattish top
    Lined inside with a slimy crop;
His mouth like a slit in a moneybox
    Portrays his kindred to a fox.
From his chin there drops a greasy beard,
    Goatlike in hue and style I've heard;
His wrinkled neck is long and thin
    To see it your sight must be in trim.

'Mickey Monkeyface McBlear'
[Mrs Ros's name for a lawyer of her acquaintance], Ibid.

I don't believe in publishers . . . I consider they're too grabby altogether. They love to keep the Sabbath and everything else they can lay their hands on.

Letters

Immoral Paris! Inside whose area are the most reprehensible dens of dignified damndom over which that immodest queen of night grins from her opalescent palace of peace, scowling over and above this abbatoir of licentiousness.

Helen Huddlestone, published 1969

W[ILLIAM] B[UTLER] YEATS (1865–1939)
He [Douglas Hyde] had much frequented the company of old countrymen, and had so acquired the Irish language, and his taste for snuff, and for moderate quantities of a detestable species of illegal whiskey distilled from a potato by certain of his neighbours.

Autobiographies, 1955

SUSAN L[ANGSTAFF] MITCHELL (1866–1926)
> I've puffed the Irish language, and puffed the Irish
>   soap;
> I've used them – on my nephew – with best
>   results, I hope.

'George Moore Crosses to Ireland',
Aids to Immortality of Certain Persons, 1908

For I took small stock in Martyn, and less in
    Douglas Hyde;
To bow to rare Æ was too much for my pride.
But W. B. was the boy for me − he of the dim,
    wan, clothes;
And − don't let on I said it − not above a bit of
    a pose;
And they call his writing literature as everybody
    knows.

Ibid.

Æ (GEORGE RUSSELL) (1867–1935)

A literary movement: five or six people who live in the same
town and hate each other.

Attrib.

LENNOX ROBINSON (1886–1958)

It is common knowledge that the leading newspapers employ
as dramatic critics journalists who are excellent on a racecourse
or a football field but who are hopelessly astray − or asleep
− in the stalls of the Gaiety or the Abbey.

A Young Man from the South, 1917

M[ICHAEL] J[OSEPH] MACMANUS (1888–1951)

    Said Dr Douglas Hyde
    'Now woe betide!
    The Gaelic League
    Is full of intrigue!'

So This Is Dublin, 1927

Mr Liam O'Flaherty
Is nothing if not hearty
But his books are lacking in national piety
According to the Catholic Truth Society.

Ibid.

It is a sad thing to see the Workhouses left lonely on the hillsides and they empty and desolate. Fine places they were surely, and grand places for talk and contention among the old people. Where will the poets and play-writers of the Abbey Theatre in Dublin be going now and the poorhouses all shut . . . The new County Homes are not the same at all, God help us, but cold respectable places not fit for a decent body to live in, having no fine talk from shuiler and tinker . . .

'The New Kiltartan History: The Workhouses' *So This Is Dublin*, 1927

'ALGOL' (F. H. ALLEN)
(EARLY-TWENTIETH CENTURY)
They soon will come, a Celtic rout,
Athirst for blood, incensed with stout,
To throw our Foreign Culture out,
    My Trinity!

    . . .

With curling lip and scornful eye,
We hear the Gaelic hue and cry,
We watch the peasants passing by,
    From Trinity!

Our sneer of cold command still quells
We've got the *savoir vivre* that tells,
We've got the blasted Book of Kells
    In Trinity!

Spirit of Cromwell! Rise again,
And subjugate by sword and pen
These rough, uncouth, untutored men
    To Trinity!

'To Trinity' in *TCD* (1943)

PATRICK KAVANAGH (1904–67)
    In their middle sits a fellow
    Aged about sixty, bland and mellow;
    Saintly silvery locks of hair,
    Quiet-voiced as a monk at prayer;
    Every Paddy's eye is glazed
    On this fellow. Mouths amazed
    Drink in all his words of praise.
    O comic muse descend to see
    The devil Mediocrity,
    For that is the devil sitting there,
    Actually Lucifer.
    . . .
    'A great renaissance is under way'
    You can hear the devil day
    As into our pub comes a new arrival
    A man who looks the conventional devil:
    This is Paddy Conscience, this

Is Stephen Dedalus,
This is Yeats who ranted to
Knave and fool before he knew,
This is Sean O'Casey saying
Fare thee well to Inishfallen . . .

'The Paddiad or The Devil as a Patron of Irish Letters', 1949

MYLES NA GOPALEEN
(BRIAN O'NOLAN, FLANN O'BRIEN) (1911–66)

Is amhlaidh a bhí:

1 *doineann na dúiche ró-dhoineanta;*

2 *bréantas na dúiche ró-bhréan;*

3 *bochtanas na dúiche ró-bhocht;*

4 *gaelachas na dúiche ró-ghaelach;*

5 *seanchas na sean ró-sheanda.*

[It appeared that;

1 The tempest of the country was too tempest uous.

2 The putridity of the countryside was too putrid.

3 The poverty of the countryside was too poor.

4 The Gaelicism of the country was too Gaelic.

5 The tradition of the country was too traditional.]

An Béal Bocht, 1941. Trans. by the author as *The Poor Mouth*, 1973

VALENTIN IREMONGER (1918–91),
BRENDAN BEHAN (1923–64) ET AL

The great voice, reminiscent of a load of gravel sliding down
the side of a quarry, booms out, the starry-eyed young poets

and painters surrounding him – all of them twenty or more years his junior, convinced (rightly too) that the Left Bank was never like this – fervently crossing themselves, there is a slackening, noticeable enough in the setting-up of the balls of malt. With a malevolent insult which, naturally, is well received the Master orders a fresh measure which produces a fit of coughing that all but stops even the traffic outside. His acolytes –sylph-like redheads, dewy-eyed brunettes, two hard-faced intellectual blondes, three rangy university poets and several semi-bearded painters – flap: 'Yous have no merit, no merit at all' – he insults them individually and collectively, they love it, he suddenly leaves to get lunch in the Bailey and have something to win on the second favourite. He'll be back.

'Patrick Kavanagh – A Profile', [unsigned] *The Leader*, October, 1952

PERSONALITIES

BISHOP PATRICK (GILLA PATRAIC) (*fl.* 1074–84)

Continet haec hominis cuiusdam terra sepulcrum
Femineas turbas fallentis more doloso
Ille etenim numerum ingentem violavit earum:
Fine tamen fuerat felici crimina deflens.
Ergo modo miro mulier, si viderit illud,
Pedere vel ridere solet cernendo sepulcrum:
Tormine iam resonat quod si non rideat illa.

De Mirabilibus Hiberniae, (c.1084)

[The land also contains the vault of one who played false with crowds of women, raping many of them. In the end, however, weeping for his vile deeds, he found forgiveness. Now strange to tell, any dame who beholds this tomb, either laughs or farts when she sees it. It makes a loud noise if the woman does not laugh.]

The Wonders of Ireland

ST OLIVER PLUNKETT (1625–81)

Sagairt óir is cailís chrainn
Bhí le linn Phádraig in Éirinn;
Sagairt chrainn is cailís óir
I ndeire an domhain dearóil.

[The priests were gold and chalices wood
In Ireland under Patrick the good;
Now the goblets are gold and priests debased
In this miserable age of sloth and waste.]

Attrib.

OLIVER GOLDSMITH (1728–74)

Magnanimous Goldsmith a gooseberry fool

Retaliation, 1774

Here lies David Garrick, describe me who can,
An abridgement of all that was pleasant in man;
. . .
On the stage he was natural, simple, affecting;
'Twas only that when he was off he was acting.
. . .
He cast off his friends, as a huntsman his pack,
For he knew when he pleas'd he could whistle
    them back.
Of praise a mere glutton, he swallowed what
    came,
And the puff of a dunce he mistook it for fame.

Ibid.

SIR BOYLE ROCHE (1743–1807)

The profligacy of the age is such that we see little children
not able to walk and talk running about the street and
cursing their Maker.

Attrib.

JOHN PHILPOT CURRAN (1750–1817)

Nothing but the head! [When asked by a barrister, 'Do you see anything ridiculous in this wig?']

Riding alone! [When asked by Lord Justice Norbury where he would be if a gallows they were passing were to have its due.]

No my lord, your lordship hasn't tried it! [When asked by Norbury if the serving was 'hung beef'.]

I have never yet heard of a murderer who was not afraid of a ghost. [To a newly ennobled Irish peer of the late parliament building in College Green.]

DANIEL O'CONNELL (1775–1847)

Peel's smile was like the silver plate on a coffin.

Attrib.

GEORGE GORDON, LORD BYRON (1788–1824)

    Posterity will ne'er survey
    A nobler grave than this.
    Here lies the bones of Castlereagh,
    Stop, traveller and piss.

Mock epitaph on Robert Stewart, Viscount Castlereagh (1769–1822),

Pitt's unpopular Irish Secretary, 1822

Who in soft guise, surrounded by a choir
Of virgins melting, not to Vesta's fire,
With sparkling eyes, and cheek by passion flush'd'
Strikes his wild lyre, whilst listening dames are
    hush'd?
'Tis Little, young Catullus of his day,
As sweet, but as immoral, in his lay.

> *English Bards and Scotch Reviewers*, 1809 [Tom Moore wrote *The*
> *Poetical Works of the late Thomas Little Esq.* in 1801.]

Good plays are scarce,
So Moore writes farce:
The poet's fame grows brittle –
We knew before that *Little*'s Moore,
But now 'tis *Moore* that's *little*.

'On Moore's last operatic farce or farcical opera', 14 September 1811

JOHN BANIM (1798–1844)

He said that he was not our brother –
    The mongrel! he said what we knew.
No, Eire! our dear Island-mother,
    He ne'er had his black blood from you!
And what though the milk of your bosom
    Gave vigour and health to his veins?
He was but a foul foreign blossom,
    Blown hither to poison our plains!

> 'He Said that He Was Not Our Brother
> [induced by some utterances of the Duke of Wellington]', 1820

R[ICHARD] R[OBERT] MADDEN (1798–1886)

'I protest as I am a gentleman . . . '

'Jintleman! Jintleman! The likes of you a jintleman! Wisha, by gor, that bangs Banagher. Why you potato-faced pippin-sneezer, when did a Madagascar monkey like you pick up enough of common Christian dacency to hide your Kerry brogue?'

'Easy now, easy now,' said O'Connell with imperturbable good humour. 'Don't choke yourself with fine language, you whiskey-drinking parallelogram.'

'What was that you called me, you murderin' villain?' roared Mrs Moriarty.

'I called you,' answered O'Connell, 'a parallelogram; and a Dublin judge and jury will say it's no libel to call you so.'

'Oh, tare-an'-ouns! Oh, Holy Saint Bridget! that an honest woman like me should be called a parrybellygrum, you rascally gallows-bird; you cowardly, sneakin' plate-lickin' blaguard!'

'Oh not you, indeed! Why, I suppose you'll deny that you keep a hypotenuse in your house.'

'It's a lie for I never had such a thing . . . '

'Why, sure all your neighbours know very well that you keep not only a hypotenuse, but that you have two diameters locked up in your garret, and that you go out to walk with them every Sunday, you heartless old heptagon.'

'Oh, hear that, ye saints in glory! Oh, there's bad language from a fellow that wants to pass for a jintleman. May the divil fly away with you, you micher from Munster, and make celery-sauce of your rotten limbs, you mealy-mouthed tub of guts.'

'Ah, you can't deny the charge, you miserable sub-multiple of a duplicate ratio.'

'Go rinse your mouth in the Liffey, you nasty tickle-pincher; after all the bad words you speak, it ought to be dirtier than your face, you dirty chicken of Beelzebub.'

'Rinse your own mouth, you wicked-minded old polygon – to the deuce I pitch you, you blustering intersection of a superficies!'

'You saucy tinker's apprentice, if you don't cease your jaw, I'll . . . ' But here she paused breath, unable to hawk up your words.

'While I have a tongue, I'll abuse you, you most inimitable periphery. Look at her, boys! There she stands – a convicted perpendicular in petticoats! There's contamination in her circumference, and she trembles with guilt down to the extremities of her corollaries. Ah, you're found out, you rectilinealantecedent and equiangular old hag! 'Tis with the devil you will fly away, you porter-swiping similitude of the bisection of a vortex!'

Overwhelmed with this torrent of language, Mrs Moriarty was silenced. Catching up a saucepan, she was aiming at O'Connell's head, while he made a timely retreat.

'Biddy Moriarty v. The Liberator' in *Revelations of Ireland*, 1877

ANON (LATE-NINETEENTH CENTURY)

May his toes fill with corns like a puckawn's horns
    Till he can neither wear slippers nor shoes,
With a horrid toothache may he roar like a drake
    And jump like a mad kangaroo.
May a horrid big rat make a hole in his hat
    And chew all the hairs off his head,
May the skin of a pig be made into a wig
And stuck on him when he is dead . . .

                '"Skin-the-Goat's" Curse on Carey' *c.* 1882

[James Carey was one of the 'Invincibles' who assassinated
Frederick Cavendish, Lord Lieutenant of Ireland and T. H.
Burke, his Under-Secretary, in the Phoenix Park on 6 May
1884. He turned Queen's evidence and implicated among
others 'Skin-the-Goat' (real name James Fitzharris), the
driver of the four-wheeler hired by him as an escape vehicle.]

THE TIMES

Scum condensed of Irish bog,
Ruffian, coward, demagogue,
Boundless liar, base detractor,
Nurse of murders, treason factor.

                Broadside against Daniel O'Connell

JOHN MITCHEL (1815–75)

Poor old Dan [O'Connell]! Wonderful, mighty, jovial and
mean old man. With silver tongue and smile of witchery and
heart of melting ruth. Lying tongue, smile of treachery,
heart of unfathomable fraud! What a royal yet vulgar soul!

With the keen eye and potent swoop of a generous eagle on Cairn Tual – with the base servility of a hound and the cold cruelty of a spider.

Jail Journal, 1854

He [O'Connell] was a lawyer; and never could come to the point of denying and defying all British law. He was a Catholic . . . and would not see that Church has ever been the enemy of Irish freedom.

Ibid.

O'Connell was, next to the British government, the worst enemy Ireland ever had – or rather the most fatal friend.

Ibid.

JOHN O'LEARY (1830–1907)
Parnell may be the Uncrowned King of Ireland; he is not the infallible Pope of Rome.

Speech at Mullinahone, August 1885

OSCAR WILDE (1854–1900)
A man who knows the price of everything and the value of nothing.

[a cynic] *Lady Windermere's Fan*: II

SOMERVILLE & ROSS
[EDITH OENONE SOMERVILLE (1858–1949)
AND VIOLET MARTIN 1862–1915)]

With the close of the 'seventies came the burst into to open of the Irish parliamentary party, in full cry. Like hounds hunting confusedly in covert, they had, in the hands of Isaac Butt, kept up a certain noise and excitement, keen, yet uncertain as to what game was on foot. From 1877 it was Parnell who carried the horn, a grim disdainful master, whose pack never dared get closer to him than the length of his thong; but he laid them on the line, and they ran like wolves.

'The Martins of Ross', *Irish Yesterdays*, 1917

JEREMIAH O'DONOVAN ROSSA (1831–1915)

Gladstone starved me till my flesh was rotten for want of nourishment, Gladstone chained me with hands behind my back for thirty-five days at a time, Gladstone leaped upon my chest while I lay on the flat of my back in a black-hole in his prison. Peori [an Italian revolutionary] didn't experience such treatment as that in an Italian prison. Yet the great Englishman could cry out his eyes for him. No wonder those eyes of his got sore in the end.

Recollections, 1838–1898, 1898

M[ICHAEL J[OSEPH] MACMANUS (1888–1951)

As to Lord Carson they do be saying that he was the cause of all the troubles in Ireland. The English gave the sway to him because he put the people in jail in the Land League days. A hard, ugly face he has on him, the Lord save us. It was in Dublin he was born, but he left there because there were too many clever people in it. That was why he went to Belfast . . .

'The New Kiltartan History: Lord Carson', *So This Is Dublin*, 1927

MICHAEL COLLINS (1890–1922)
The long 'hoor [his soubriquet for de Valera].

Passim.

Chirruping birds. This is a real nest of chirruping birds. They chirrup mightily one to the other – and there's the falseness of it, because not one trusts the other.

Letter to John O'Kane, 23 October 1921, describing some of the early moves in the Treaty negotiations.

'THE BELLMAN'
A stage Irishman about town.

'Meet Patrick Kavanagh' *The Bell*: XVI, i, April 1948

JAMES DILLON (1902–86)
You're not a pheasant; you're nothing but a phartridge!
[Dáil response to a TD who kept mispronouncing 'peasant']

Attrib.

CONOR CRUISE O'BRIEN (*b.* 1917)
If I saw Mr Haughey buried at midnight at a cross-roads, with a stake through his heart – politically speaking – I should continue to wear a clove of garlic round my neck, just in case.

The Observer, 10 October 1982

Worse than the Men?

St Columbanus (*c.* 543–615)

Caveto, filole,
Feminarum species,
Per quas mors ingreditur;
Non parva pernicies.

[Beware, my son, womenkind by whom death
enters; no small danger.]

De Mundi Transitu [*The Passing of Earthly Things*]

Anon (Fifteenth Century0

Fuge cetus feminarum
Namque status omnis harum
Parva dat stipendia.
Si sit virgo, quam tu gliscis
Dampna rerum concupiscis
Cordia et incendia.
Maritatam si tu amas
Pacem spernis, te defamas
Incendis periculum.
Vidua haec est elata
Fraude plena, delictata
Eris ei ridiculum.
Monialis hec si placet
semper petit, numquam tacet
Radit ut navicula.

Si bagute facieris
Mox per eam diffameris
    Linguam fierit ut facula.

[Shun the shoals of pushy women;
Having too much interest in them
    Gives very poor returns.
If a virgin you should favour
Over which to fawn and slaver –
    Heartbreak and finger-burns!
If a married dame you're wooing
She'll prove to be your last undoing,
    Spitted down in hell!
Tricky widows take the biscuit;
For a lad like you they'll risk it:
    Lampoon you as well.
And nuns are always on the go,
Deafening, chugging to and fro,
    Boats without a bung.
Even a whore's not worth the candle
Soon the town will ring with scandal
    Lit by flaming tongue!]

AN T-ATHAIR SEATHRÚN CÉITINN
(1580–c. 1644)

A bhean lán de stuaim
  coingibh uaim do lámh:
ní fear gníomha sinn,
  cé taoi tinn dar ngrádh

Féach ar liath dem fholt,
  féach mo chorp gan lúth,
féach ar traoch dem fhuil—
  créad re bhfuil do thnúth.

[Jade, that's banned!
Remove that hand!
I'm just not fit
Though you're mad for it!

Look: hair's grey;
Desire won't stay;
My blood runs thin.
Yet you want to play?]

'A Bhean Lán de Stuaim' ['Woman, full of tricks']

ANON (SEVENTEENTH CENTURY)

Taisigh agat féin do phóg,
  a ingean óg is geal déad;
ar do phóig ní bhfagaim blas.
  Congaibh uaim amach do bhéal.

78

[Keep your kiss,
White-toothed miss.
It has no flavour;
Withdraw your favour!]

'Taisigh Agat Féin Do Phóg' ['Keep Your Kiss to Yourself']

Ní bhfuighe mise bás duit
  a bhean úd an cuirp mar ghéis;
daoine leamha ar mharbhais riamh
  ní hionnan iad is mé féin.

[Madam, I won't die for you
Though bodied like a swan;
Weaker guys you may have stilled;
I ain't that kind of John!]

'Ní Bhfuige Mise Bás Duit' ['I Will Not Die for You']

Do dhúisceocadh mairbh a huaigh
  leis gach fuaim dá dtig ód shróin;
a chaomhthaigh luigheas im ghar,
  is doiligh dhamh bheith dod chóir.

[The dead might wake from their graves
With each honk that comes from your nose.
Old mate that lie by my side,
No wonder I'm feeling morose!]

'Ní Binn Do Thorann lem Thaoibh' ['The noise at my side is not pleasant']

JONATHAN SWIFT (1667–1745)

'Twixt earthly females and the moon
All parallels exactly run;
If Celia should appear too soon
Alas, the nymph would be undone.

. . .

To see her from her pillow rise
All reeking in a cloudy steam,
Crack'd lips, foul teeth, and gummy eyes,
Poor Strephon, how would he blaspheme!

'The Progress of Beauty', 1719

Then, Chloe, still go on to prate
Of thirty-six and thirty-eight;
Pursue your trade of scandal-picking.
Your hints that Stella is no chicken;
Your innuendoes, when you tell us,
That Stella loves to talk with fellows;
Let me warn you to believe
A truth, for which your soul should grieve;
That should you live to see the day
When Stella's locks must all be gray,
When age must print a furrowed trace
On every feature of her face;
Though you, and all your senseless tribe,
Could Art, or Time, or Nature bribe,
To make you look like Beauty's Queen,
And hold for ever at fifteen;
No bloom of youth, can ever blind

The cracks and wrinkles of your mind:
And men of sense will pass your door
And crowd to Stella's at four-score.

'Stella's Birthday', 1720

SUSANNAH CENTILIVRE (*c.* 1667–1723)
The carping malice of the vulgar world; who think it proof
of sense to dislike every thing that is written by a woman.

Dedication, *The Platonic Lady,* 1707

Nothing to be done without a bribe I find, in love as well
as law.

The Perjured Husband: III, ii, 1700

For he or she who drag the marriage chain,
And find in spouse occasion to complain,
Should hide their frailties with a lover's care
And let th'ill-judging world conclude 'em fair;
Better th'offence ne'er reach th'offender's ear
For they who sin with caution, whilst concealed,
Grow impudently careless, when revealed.

The Artifice: V, iii, 1722

SIR RICHARD STEELE (1672–1729)
Will Honeycomb calls these over-offended ladies the
outrageously virtuous.

The Spectator, no. 266, 4 January 1712

MARY BARBER (1690–1757)

Her husband has surely a terrible life;
There's nothing I dread, like a verse-writing wife:
Defend me, ye powers, from that fatal curse
Which must heighten the plagues of *for better or
worse*!

'Conclusion of a Letter to the Rev Mr C-', 1734

KANE O'HARA (1714–82)

APOLLO: Pray, goody, please to moderate your tongue;
Why flash those sparks of fury from your eyes?
Remember, when the judgement's weak, the
prejudice is strong.

Midas: I, *iv*, 1761

THOMAS MOORE (1779–1852)

There *was* a time, falsest of women!
When Breffni's good sword would have sought
That man, through a million of foemen,
Who dared but to doubt thee *in thought!*
While now – O degenerate daughter
Of Erin, how fallen is thy fame!
And, through ages of bondage and slaughter
Thy country shall bleed for thy shame.

'The Song of O'Ruark, Prince of Breffni', 1808

ANON (NINETEENTH CENTURY)

A Ghearalit ghéir an gháire ghreanta,
fásach go raibh go tairseach do gheata,
driseog is a dhá cheann sa talamh,
loch uaine ar uachtar do halla,
nead an tseabhaic i bpoll an deataigh,
agus fail na ngabhar ag ceann do leapa.

[Detestable Gerald with your studied smile,
May dry desert waste your threshold defile,
Double brambles infest your land overall
And a lake of green scum disfigure your hall.
May your chimney be host to a hawk and its nest
And a goat have his fold in your pallet of rest.]

'Mallacht na Baintrí' ['The Widow's Curse']

An áit a mbíonn toit bíonn tine,
An áit a mbíonn tine bíonn teas,
An áit a mbíonn teas bíonn mná
An áit a mbíonn mná bíonn gab.

[No smoke without fire;
No fire without heat;
No heat without women;
No women without tweet.]

Seanfhocal [proverb]

For she's a big stout lump of an agricultural Irish
    girl
She neither paints nor powders and her figure is
    all her own
And she can strike that hard that you'd think that
    you'd been struck by the kick of a mule
It's 'the full of the house' of Irish love is Mary Ann
    Malone.

'The Agricultural Irish Girl'

So it's true that the women are worse than the
    men
For they went down to Hell and were threw out
    again!

'Killyburn Brae'

May his pig never grunt, may his cat never hunt,
May a ghost ever haunt him at dead of the
    night;
May his hen never lay, may his ass never bray,
May his goat fly away like an old paper kite.
That the flies and the fleas may the wretch ever
    tease,
And the piercing north wind make him shiver
    and shake,

May a lump of a stick raise bumps fats and thick
On the monster that murdered Nell Flaherty's
     drake.

'Nell Flaherty's Drake'

Here lies, praise God, a woman who
Scolded and stormed her whole life through:
Tread gently o'er her rotting form
Or else you'll raise another storm.

In Raymond Lamont-Brown, *Grave Humour*, 1987

OSCAR WILDE (1854–1900)
The amount of women in London who flirt with their own
husbands is perfectly scandalous. It looks so bad. It is simply
washing one's clean linen in public.

The Importance of Being Earnest: I

KATHERINE TYNAN (1861–1931)
     Margaret Grady – I fear she will burn –
     Charmed the butter off my churn.

J[OHN] M[ILLINGTON] SYNGE (1871–1909)
     Lord, confound this surly sister,
     Blight her brow with blotch and blister,
     Cramp her larynx, lungs and liver,
     In her guts a galling give her.

'The Curse', *Poems and Translations*, 1911

W[ILLIAM] F[REDERICK] MARSHALL (1888–1959)
>   ... her face was like a gaol dure
>   With the bowlts pulled out.

'Me an' Me Da', 1929

TOM [THOMAS BERNARD] MURPHY (*b.* 1935)
... that hussy of a clotty of a plótha of a streleen of an ownshock of a lebidjeh of a girleen that's working above in the bank.

A Crucial Week in the Life of a Grocer's Assistant, 1969

ANTHONY CLARE (*b.* 1945)
The whole notion of holding a referendum on women's access to information is such a profound disgrace for a nation such as this that I ... apologise to Irish women on behalf of what has been a male-dominated, male-driven male disgrace.

The Irish Times, 8 January 1993

MOTHER CHURCH

ANON (FOURTEENTH CENTURY)

When the summer day is hot,
All the young nuns take a boat
And goeth on the river clear,
Row with oars, with rudder steer.
When far enought from all the abbey,
They make them naked for to play
And leapeth down into the brim
And starteth timidly to swim.
The young monks when the nuns they see
Get them up and forth they flee
And cometh to the nuns anon,
And every monk he taketh one,
And slyly beareth forth their prey
Unto the abbey great and grey,
And teach the nuns an orison
With an ambling up and down.

'The Land of Cokagne' [modern version by Russell K. Alspach]

ANON (SEVENTEENTH CENTURY)

Ná thrácht ar an mhinistéir Gallda,
Ná ar a chreideamh gan bheann, gan bhrí
Mar níl mar buan-chloch dá theampuill
Ach magairle Annraoi, Rí.

[Don't speak of the alien minister,
Nor of his church without meaning or faith,
For the foundation stone of his temple
Is the ballocks of Henry the Eighth.]

Quoted and translated in Brendan Behan, Borstal Boy, 1958

JOHN WINSTANLEY (1678–1750)

Cries Celia to a reverend dean,
'What reason can be given,
Since marriage is a holy thing,
That there are none in heaven?'
'There are no women,' he replied;
She quick returns the jest;
'Women there are, but I'm afraid
They cannot find a priest.'

'On Marriage', Poems, 1742

OLIVER GOLDSMITH (1730–74)

Almost every fountain in this country is under the patronage of some saint, where the people once a year meet to show their strength and best clothes, drink muddy ale, dance with each other's mistresses, get drunk, beat each other with cudgels most unmercifully. These religious meetings are never known to pass without bloodshed and battery, and their priests often put themselves at the head of opposite parties, and gain more renown in cudgel-playing than in piety.

'A Description of the Manners and Customs of the Native Irish', 1759

THOMAS MOORE (1797–1852)
Your priests, whate'er their gentle shamming
Have always had a taste for damning.

Intercepted Letters, or The Two-penny Post Bag, 1813

ANON (NINETEENTH CENTURY)
    Scarlet Church of all uncleanness,
    Sink thou to the deep abyss,
    To the orgies of obsceneness,
    Where the hell-bound furies hiss;
    Where thy father Satan's eye
    May hail thee, blood-stained Papacy.

'The Papacy' (Orange ballad)

GERALD [JEREMIAH] O'DONOVAN (1871–1942)
The Carmelites will do their best to get him. He would be
wasted on them – the boy ought to be a scholar, not a pulpit
windbag.

Father Ralph, 1913

SEAN O'FAOLAIN (1900–91)
I was in fact exactly forty-six years old before I finally
abandoned the faith of my fathers, and, under the live-loving
example of Italy, became converted to Roman Catholicism.

'A Portrait of the Artist as an Old Man', *Irish University Review*, 1976

IRISH HIERARCHY
During the intervals the devil is busy; yes very busy, as sad
experience proves, and on the way home in the small hours

of the morning he is busier still

Statement on late-night dancing, *Irish Catholic*, 23 December 1933

NOËL BROWNE (*b.* 1915)

No one can seriously doubt but that the Catholic Church has behaved to all our political parties in an identical way as the Orange Order in its control of the Unionist Party in the North – a sectarian and bigoted politically conservative pressure group.

The Irish Times, 1 May 1971

BERNADETTE DEVLIN [MCALISKEY] (*b.* 1947)

Among the best traitors Ireland has ever had, Mother Church ranks at the very top, a massive obstacle in the path of equality and freedom.

The Price of My Soul, 1969

PROTESTANTS WITH HORSES

ANONYMOUS (FOURTEENTH CENTURY)

... now many English of the said land, forsaking the English language, fashion, manner of riding, laws and customs, live and govern themselves by the manners, fashion and language of the Irish enemies.

Statutes of Kilkenny, 1366 [language modernised]

AN TATHAIR PÁDRAIGÍN HAICÉAD (*c.* 1600–54)

Is cor do leag mé cleas an phlás-tsaoilse
mogh in gach teach ag fear an smáilBhéarla
's gan scot ag neach le fear den dáimh éigse
ach 'hob amach 's beir leat do sharGhaelgsa.'

[The cheating world has played me a foul trick;
The churls of landlords speaking English dung
Respect no poet, and cry crudely, 'Mick:
Out with you and your precious Gaelic tongue!']

'Faisean Chláir Éibhir" [The fashion on Eibhear's Plain]

WENTWORTH DILLON,
FOURTH EARL OF ROSCOMMON (1633–85)

The multitude is always in the wrong.

Essay on Translated Verse, 1684

Aogán Ó Rathaille (c. 1675–1729)

Do thonnchrith m'inchinn, d'imigh mo príomhdóchas,
poll im ionathar, biora nimhe trím dhrólainn,
ár bhfonn, ár bhfothain, ar monga 's ár mínchóngair
i ngeall le pinginn ag foirinn ó chrích Dhóbhair.

[My head's all at sea, my best hope is gone;
My entrails are spiked; the pain turns me over;
Our basis, our refuge, our portion, our roads
Are hocked for a cent by the bagmen from Dover.]

'Cabhair Ní Ghairfead' ['I'll not cry for help']

Seán Clárach Mac Dónaill (1691–1754)

Brúigh, leac, a dhraid 's a dhrandal crón
A shúile, a phlait, a theanga, a tholl dubh mór,
gach lúith, gach alt, go prap den chamshliteoir,
mar shúil ná casfaidh tar ais ná a shamhailt go deo.

Cé go rabhais-se mustarach iomarcach santach riamh,
biaidh do chiste 'ge cimire gann id dhiaidh,
do cholann ag cruimhe dá poicadh go hamplach dian
is t'anam ag fiuchadh sa gcoire gan contas blian.

[His sneer, yellow gums, all now turning to mush,
Eyes, skull and tongue, and massive black anus,
Every joint, every sinew, good gravestone, all
    crush
So that ne'er may be seen his duplicate heinous.

Though arrogant, boastful and mean all your days,
Your riches shall all go to skinflints of heirs.
Your corpse will be nibbled by worms in relays,
Your soul cooked in the cauldron for millions of
    years.]

'Taiscidh, a Chlocha – Ar bhás Shéamais Dawson'
[Hold Fast, Stones – on the Death of James Dawson'
(a hated Aherlow landlord)]

ANON (EIGHTEENTH CENTURY)

Do threascair an saol is shéid an ghaoth mar smál
Alastrann, Caesar, 'an méid sin a bhí 'na bpáirt;
tá an Teamair 'na féar is féach an Traoi mar tá,
is na Sasanaigh féin do bfhéidir go bhfaighidis bás.

[Time has laid low and the breeze blown like dust
Alexander and Caesar and all of their host.
Tara's a hayfield and Troy's had its day
Even the English may dwindle away.]

ARTHUR YOUNG (1741–1820)

[Irish landlords] . . . lazy, trifling, inattentive, negligent,
slobbering, profligate.

A Tour of Ireland, 1780

BERNARD SHAW (1856–1950)

. . . the Irish squire takes the title deeds of the English
settlement and rises uncovered to the strains of the English
national anthem. But do not mistake this cupboard loyalty

for anything deeper.

Preface to *John Bull's Other Island*, 1906

SOMERVILLE & ROSS
[EDITH OENONE SOMERVILLE (1858–1949)
AND VIOLET MARTIN (1862–1915)

There wasn't a day in the year you wouldn't get feeding for a hen and chickens on the floor.

'Philippa's Fox-Hunt', *Some Experiences of an Irish RM* (1899)

LOUIS MACNEICE (1907–1963)

In most cases these houses maintained no culture worth speaking of – nothing but an obsolete bravado, an insidious bonhomie and a way with horses.

The Poetry of W. B. Yeats, 1941

BRENDAN BEHAN (1923–64)

PAT: He was an Anglo-Irishman
MEG: In the blessed name of God what's that?
PAT: A Protestant with a horse.

The Hostage, Act One, 1958

The myth of the Anglo-Irish would have us believe that the most rapacious rack-renting landlord-class in Europe were really lamps of culture in a bog of darkness, doing good by stealth and shoving copies of *Horizon* under the half-doors of the peasantry after dark and making wedding presents to the cottagers of Ganymede Press reproductions of Gauguin.

Brendan Behan's Island, 1962

INDEX OF AUTHORS